Bitcoin Basics: Buying, Selling, Creating and Investing Bitcoins – The Digital Currency of the Future

BENJAMIN TIDEAS

ISBN: 1508478945
ISBN-13: 978-1508478942

CONTENTS

INTRODUCTION

I want to thank you and congratulate you on grabbing the book, "Bitcoin Basics: Buying, Selling, Creating and Investing Bitcoins – The Digital Currency of the Future".

This book contains proven steps and strategies for understanding and getting started using Bitcoins. It also contains tips on how to avoid possible pitfalls in case you decide to put some good money into it.

Bitcoin has created such a huge impact on people's economic perspectives in such a short time that it is worthwhile to educate yourself about possibly making an investment.

Thanks again for picking up this book, I hope you enjoy it!

Also, Don't forget to grab your FREE Bonuses via the link at the end!

Now, let's get to it!

WHAT IS BITCOIN AND HOW DOES IT WORK?

Bitcoin is the first ever peer-to-peer digital currency created to facilitate online payments without the need of coursing the transactions through a financial institution. It is an electronic cash system designed to be the medium of exchange in the burgeoning internet commerce. Bitcoin has no physical attributes because it is purely a digital currency. There are no minted tokens or printed paper money to represent its value. Instead, it is an encoded algorithm (a 'hash', or a string of data) that is encrypted to represent one unit of currency.

There is no central authority that regulates Bitcoin. Instead, it uses cryptography to manage its creation and its transfer from one user to another. Management of the various transactions is a collective effort of the network.

Bitcoin is virtual money and like all other currencies in the world has its own stored value. Its value, however is not backed by gold or other precious commodities like the currencies of gold. It is more like fiat currency (similar to the U.S. Dollar) which the issuing government money declares as legal tender despite not being backed by its weight in gold or silver. As fiat currencies that have values derived from the holder's faith in the countries issuing them, Bitcoins also derive their values from the holders' faith in the global digital network that oversees it.

Like fiat currencies, Bitcoins become acceptable as payment for goods and services simply because people have confidence on the issuing authority, which in this case is the Bitcoin network populated by users who believe in it. The bottom-line - as a peer-to-peer currency, the real value of the Bitcoin depends on how much of it the seller will be willing to part with his goods or services and how much of it the buyer will be willing to pay.

Bitcoin is described best as a crypto-currency that is purely digital, totally peer-to-peer, uncontrolled and unregulated by any central authority, and cannot be controlled nor regulated by any government. This only exists in your computers, smart phones, and tablets yet this still has the same buying power and value as any other currency.

How the Bitcoin System Works (For the Geeks)

Bitcoin is an electronic cash system that is dependent on and makes use of three essential elements to manage its creation and process and verify its every use. The vital elements are peer-to-peer networking, public key cryptography, and proof of work.

Peer-to-peer networking means it has no central authority to manage the operations and the responsibility of processing data and transactions shared by everyone connected to the network. Public key cryptography indicates it uses two different keys – a private key which is used to create a digital signature, and a public key which is used to verify the digital signature. Proof of work is a system used to prevent denial of service attacks – it comes in the form of a string of data that is difficult and tough to produce but once produced, affirms that the work was done.

Bitcoin circulation is fixed at 21,000,000 total digital coins which will be embedded (distributed) into the Bitcoin network nodes in batches with the number of coins to be cut in half every four years as follows: 10,500,000 – first; 5,250,000 – second; 2,625,000 – third; and so on. These coins will be released into the system through a process called 'mining' which will be discussed in detail, in another chapter of this book. To date, approximately 12,000,000 Bitcoins have been introduced into circulation since the first release in January 9, 2009.

They call the process of creating or retrieving the embedded Bitcoins 'mining' because, like miners, network users have to exert great effort to solve the difficult mathematical problems and create blocks before they are rewarded with the release of the new Bitcoins from the network nodes. Anyone can 'mine' for Bitcoins by using a free application called 'Bitcoin Miner' which can be downloaded for free from the Bitcoin website.

Every new Bitcoin introduced into the network originally comes from mining, and given as a form of reward for block solutions to successful miners. Mining is solving a block of Bitcoin transactions by looking for a hash or a string of values that fits the network's stringent cryptographic rules. It is like solving a cryptographic puzzle. It may require several attempts before you are able to solve a block. Also, the level of difficulty increases as more of the Bitcoins go into circulation.

The, Bitcoin 'miners' are essentially taking part in a collective effort designed to create a distributed consensus to confirm every Bitcoin transaction. In exchange for their efforts, miners are rewarded with new Bitcoins (at the time of this writing: 25 coins per block of transactions successfully processed or solved).

This is pretty much how the embedded Bitcoins are dug up, created, or generated and introduced into the system for the first time. Thereafter, every time a Bitcoin changes hands, its digital signature is invalidated, and a new digital signature is assigned which in effect, destroys the old coin and creates a new one in the same place.

How the Bitcoin System Works (For the Less Geeky)

Even without understanding the technical details surrounding Bitcoin, a user can just as easily start using it simply by downloading and installing his own Bitcoin wallet on his desktop or any mobile device. Installing the Bitcoin wallet software will generate an address for you and you can create as many wallets as you want. You can now store the Bitcoins you purchased or received as payments in your wallet. To receive payment, you simply share your Bitcoin address with your friends or clients, and they can send their payments to this address, which is pretty much like sending email. It is as simple as that.

If you intend to install a Bitcoin wallet on your desktop, you can download the Multibit installer online. If you want to install a wallet on your smart phone or other mobile devices, then you can also download the Bitcoin Wallet installer for androids.

Where Can You Use Bitcoins?

With Bitcoins stashed in your wallet, all you need now is to find vendors who'll accept them as payment. Like any other commodity, Bitcoins can be exchanged, bought, or sold. They can be used to buy goods or procure services from a growing number of shops that directly accept them, and they are spread out all across the globe and used by online shops as well as brick and mortar stores. You can buy anything from pizza to clothing, to electronic gadgets, etc. using Bitcoins today. Or you can simply exchange them for cash. You can also make use of related services such as Bitspend or Bitpay to purchase from the biggest online stores to the smallest online stores.

THE HISTORY OF BITCOIN

The idea of creating a digital currency came about for the first time in 1992 after a group of scientists headed by retired Intel physicist, Timothy May, met to discuss the issue of privacy and the then infantile internet which various governments around the world wanted to rein in. Specifically, the government wanted to prevent the use of cryptographic protocols that insure privacy on the internet. The group called itself the Cypherpunks.

A lot of ideas on how to keep the internet private, independent and free from government regulatory measures were floated around. One of them, Jim Bell, floated the idea of creating a digital coin, but it was for a purpose totally unrelated to privacy issues. It was to solicit donations to fund assassination plots against government officials who go against the will of the people, and set up an anarchic end which most in the group did not approve of.

Another cypherpunk member, a computer scientist by the name of Nick Szabo, proposed the creation of bit-gold, a digital currency which shall be free from intervention by any central authority and to be created from the ground up. He wanted bit-gold to serve as an alternative to the mainstream currencies.

It was Szabo who first floated the idea of encouraging users to solve puzzles and to reward those who can come up with solutions with the digital coins. In his Bitgold proposal, users will be encouraged to compete against each other to solve a string of challenge bits using the proof of work function (also known as secure benchmark functions). Unfortunately, his idea found no fruition since it encountered a lot of technical difficulties.

In 1998, at about the same time Szabo's Bitgold proposal was published, another cypherpunk, Wei Dai, a fresh graduate from the University of Washington published yet another proposal for creating B-money, a crypto-currency that in essence was a distributed electronic cash system.

Unfortunately, both Nick Szabo's Bitgold and Wei Dai's B-money failed to generate support and could not get off the ground. Nothing about a digital currency was ever heard of for the next ten years. And when people were starting to think that the idea of an alternative digital currency have all but fizzled out, an email from a Satoshi Nakamoto containing a paper entitled "Bitcoin: A Peer-to-Peer Electronic Cash System" was sent to a cryptography mailing list on November 1, 2008, which had everyone talking. The discussion thread from this email grew extremely fast and included prominent figures in the mailing list such as Hal Finney.

Barely three months after this email, on January 9, 2009, Nakamoto released Bitcoin v0.1 to the same mailing list officially launching Bitcoin. On January 12, 2009, the first Bitcoin transaction was made involving 50 coins sent by Nakamoto to Hal Finney. On October 5, 2009, the first rate of exchange between Bitcoin and the USD was published by New Liberty Standard, which was pegged at $1 = 1,309.03 Bitcoins.

Bitcoins started with the value of mere pennies but quickly rose thereafter. The value rose in popularity as more and more entities began accepting it. In 2011, it hit the peak of $32 to buy one Bitcoin rising from the mere $0.30 value it had at the start. It amazingly hit a high of $1230 momentarily in 2012 and has settled at an average of $235.00 today. Occasionally, speculators have shown great interest and entered the fray pushing the price of a Bitcoin to record highs in the Bitcoin exchanges. At current writing, it is trading around $250.

BUYING AND SELLING BITCOINS

You need to have a Bitcoin wallet first before you can buy or sell Bitcoins. The Bitcoin wallet is where the coins are received and sent, without which a transaction won't push through. Creating a Bitcoin wallet is easy. All you need to do is download a Bitcoin client application and run it.

There are 3 types of Bitcoin wallet applications available:

- Some of the more popular software wallets include Multibit, Blockchain.info, Bitcoin Core, and Armory. Software wallets are those that you install on desktops. With software wallets, you maintain complete control and responsibility of your money including protecting it from being hacked and creating back up files.
- Mobile wallets such as the Bitcoin Wallet for android, for example, are available on Google Play. Mobile wallets are installed on your mobile device or smartphones. This means you can bring your Bitcoins everywhere you go and use them at any brick and mortar stores that accept Bitcoins. To pay using your mobile wallet, you would simply scan the QR code or use the NFC 'tap to pay' application.
- Online wallets are hosted Bitcoin wallets, the most popular being Coinbase. You'd be able to use them anywhere that there is internet access. However, since third party hosting services will keep your bitcoins, you need to be extra careful in choosing the most trustworthy among them.

You can download the Multibit installer online for free if you are installing your wallet on a desktop. If you want to install a wallet on your smart phone or other mobile devices, then you can download the Bitcoin Wallet installer for androids at Google Play.

With a Bitcoin wallet, you can now start acquiring and transacting Bitcoins. You can now accept them as payment for the goods or services you offer if you are into some kind of business. If you want to obtain more Bitcoins, you can go to any of the existing Bitcoin Exchanges. But of course, the easiest way to obtain Bitcoins is to buy them from someone you know who has them. Or, you can also get them for free as offers or bonuses from some online shops and gaming applications as an incentive for your purchase and/or patronage.

Please note that Bitcoin exchanges do not accept credit card or PayPal payments. This is because they can easily arbitrarily reverse payments which will leave the Bitcoins in the hands of the buyer, who can surreptitiously get his money back via a chargeback by filing a concocted complaint. It may be possible to find people who will sell Bitcoins in exchange for a credit card or PayPal payment, but your best bet is to buy from the exchange and pay instead via money transfer services.

INVESTING IN BITCOINS

The Bitcoin economy may still be in its infancy stage, but the value of the Bitcoins in circulation today is roughly estimated at around $2 billion and continues to rise rapidly. On top of that, budding services that will beef up the Bitcoin economy are sprouting like mushrooms all over the world. It will be hard not to notice a growing number of techno-geeks who dedicate their time, money, and skills in developing digital wallet applications, creating Bitcoin payment processors, building Bitcoin exchanges - all in support of establishing a robust Bitcoin ecosystem.

Inescapable too is the increasing number of establishments from every corner of the globe, online or otherwise, that are now accepting Bitcoins alongside the US Dollar, the Euro, and the Yen as payment for traditional goods and services. With people growing wary of the high fees being charged on credit card transactions, and their developing distrust for the banking institution all over the world in the heels of the JP Morgan debacle and other scandals involving prominent financial institutions, Bitcoin just may be viewed as the best safe haven for valuable capital, next to gold.

The Huge Potential of Bitcoin

Financial experts agree that the potential for growth of Bitcoin is huge and unfathomable as of this time. Some of them even believe it can replace gold calling it Gold 2.0. Compared to gold, this crypto-currency is easy to use for any transaction, and it will cost you nothing to store it, not to mention the fact that it is free from the regulatory manipulations of any government or central authority.

When it was first introduced in 2009, Bitcoin costs only $0.30 each. As of this writing, it's trading above $250, briefly touching the $400 level, and still poised for more upward vertical movement. But the question in everybody's mind is how far up it can go?

Believe it or not but there are financial experts who pegged the value of Bitcoin at $400,000 each! And if you are wondering how they came up with this seemingly scandalous figure, well, it came up with the assumption that Bitcoin will in due time replace gold. By extrapolating the current value of all the gold in the world ($8 trillion) to the total number of Bitcoins (21,000,000) that will be in circulation, you'll come up with $400,000 ($8 trillion divided by 21,000,000 Bitcoins. This serves as the upper limits of the potential value of Bitcoins, and that is just for starters. Who knows how much more it can appreciate in value if some countries start using it as their reserve currency, which incidentally is not too far-fetched.

But, hold your horses! Before you take the plunge and place all your investible funds into Bitcoins, you must consider the fact that this is an emerging technology, and it would be inadvisable to throw caution to the wind. The more experienced investors who believe there are bright prospects for this virtual currency in the future are timidly placing their investments in it, limiting their exposure to Bitcoins to no more than 1% of their portfolio. You should too. It would be disastrous to consider investing on Bitcoins as a get-rich-quick scheme.

So, how do you invest on Bitcoins?

Buying and selling Bitcoins is easy. There are a number of Bitcoin exchanges where you can buy or sell Bitcoins much like the stock market where buy orders are matched with existing sell orders. The prices of Bitcoins are quoted on real time basis depending on the latest price it is currently trading.

If you want a more stable pricing plan, you can go to a fixed rate Bitcoin broker instead. These are the small Bitcoin buy and sell merchants who make money by putting a small spread between buying and selling prices.

Then there are   bulk Bitcoin buyers who only buy and sell the coins in amounts of $10,000 or higher. They are the liquidity providers in the Bitcoin investment landscape.

Don't blink now but there are also physical Bitcoins you can buy. Physical Bitcoins are actual bearer tokens with an embedded Bitcoin value that can only be redeemed if the coin is torn open. This is one of the easiest ways to accumulate Bitcoins because you can use PayPal or even your credit card to purchase these coins.

However, whichever way you chose to acquire Bitcoins, it is necessary to exert extra effort to determine the real world identity of the dealers or the operators of the exchange before sending your money to any of them. Trading in Bitcoins is highly unregulated, and there is a high risk you may end up dealing with an unscrupulous operator who will abscond with your money.

It is best to visit their websites and get to know the people behind the company first. You can also browse various Bitcoin forums with an eye for any negative feedback from previous users of the Bitcoin exchanges with whom you are considering transacting.

MINING BITCOINS

Mining is the process that ensures the integrity and efficiency of the Bitcoin system. Mining serves a three-fold function – (1) To process Bitcoin Transactions, (2) Secure the Bitcoin network, and (3) Keep everyone in the system synchronized with one another.

The best way to understand is to compare it to gold. Gold is rare or in limited supply, and it derives its value from the fact that people want it. Like gold, the supply of Bitcoin is limited (capped at 21,000,000 coins). It also has value because people give them value for numerous reasons.

The most important analogy is that gold is produced by mining them and similarly Bitcoins are produced through a process called mining. The only difference while you dig dirt for the gold, with Bitcoin, the mining is purely a mathematical process.

A total of 21,000,000 Bitcoins have been distributed (or embedded) to the Bitcoin network nodes. In order to 'dig up' the Bitcoins, participants (called miners) will have to pack a group of Bitcoin transactions into a block and then search for a string of data that matches a particular pattern when the Bitcoin cryptographic hash is applied to it. Whoever is first to make a match for a particular block unlocks a bunch of Bitcoins (currently at 25) as his reward or bounty. The bounty becomes smaller while the level of difficulty increases as more and more of the Bitcoins are unlocked. It can be likened to looking for prime numbers where it will be easy to find the smaller primes but becomes exceedingly difficult as you progress into the larger numbers.

Here is the sequence of events for Bitcoin mining:

1. When new Bitcoin transactions occur, they are promptly transmitted to all the Bitcoin network nodes.
2. A miner collects new transactions that enters his node and packs them into a block.
3. He then starts searching for that matching string of data that will be the proof-of-work for his block.
4. When a miner discovers a proof-of-work, the solved block is immediately broadcasted to all the other nodes in the network.
5. New Bitcoins are then released to the node of the miner who found the proof-of-work first.
6. The system as a whole accepts the block only after majority of the nodes agree that all transactions in it are valid, and none of the Bitcoins involved have already been spent.
7. Acceptance of the block is confirmed by the creation of the next block in the chain where the algorithm value of the accepted block becomes the hash of the previous block.

As you may have noticed, the Bitcoin 'miners' are essentially taking part in a collective effort designed to generate a distributed consensus to confirm every Bitcoin transaction. At the same time, they strengthen the integrity of the network as well as ensure that everybody is synchronized with one another.

To Mine or Not to Mine

Mining requires a great deal of computing power to process the increasing number of transactions. Much more so because the level of difficulty has increased to the point that it now requires billions of calculations per second to produce a single proof of work. On top of that, more miners are joining the fray. Many of them are equipped with more powerful GPUs (Graphics Processing Units) or gaming computers that are a thousand times more powerful than the regular CPUs.

Others have even built supercomputers dedicated to Bitcoin mining using the ASICs (Application Specific Integrated Circuits), which is the same technology used in modern cellphones and other mobile devices. Mining Bitcoins all by your lonesome self using a regular computer will only make you eat the dust of the more sophisticated miners. It will take you ages to be able to solve a block. Remember, it is a game of who gets to solve a block first.

Your best bet if you want to go Bitcoin mining at this point in time is to join mining pools. A mining pool combines the computing power of a group of miners with the work divided among them. Everyone gets a share of the bounty from every solved block commensurate to the amount of work he has contributed.

The only problem with pool mining is the possibility of the pool operator absconding with your Bitcoin bounty and keeping them for himself. While this is something that can't be discounted, the risk can be minimized by making a careful choice. It is best that before joining any mining pool, you should scan the various Bitcoin mining forums to look for mining pools with positive feedbacks and stay away from those with unacceptable comments.

There are now Cloud Mining sites that will, in essence, rent you the computational power required to mine bitcoins. Since it is quite difficult to harness the required amount of power to mine on one's own. Instead of adding your machine to the pool, you rent someone else's anonymous machine to do the mining for you. It is easier than it sounds, and probably the most realistic way to get into Bitcoin mining for the first time.

To get you started here is a list of top Bitcoin Mining Pools (with Links!) you may consider researching/joining:

- CEX.IO - For Cloud Mining, you actually purchase GHS, or Bitcoin cloud mining power, according to market price, and your GHS will start mining for you immediately. With CEX.IO, you can sell your GHS at any time, or even trade them for fiat money or crypto-currencies and make a profit.
- BTC Guild - BTC Guild is one of the pioneering Bitcoin Mining Pools, which still operates as of writing and tops everyone else, accounting for 30% of the total blocks found for 2013. It provides a simple but feature-filled interface for its users.
- Slush Pool- aka MiningBitcoinCZ – accounts for 10% of the total blocks found in 2013. It was the first mining pool created and has been in operation since December, 2010. It boasts of having a consistent and stable payout since the start of its operations.
- Bit minter – accounts for 5% of total blocks found for 2013. It boasts of having an innovative, gauge metered mining software which runs with just one click.
- Eclipse – accounts for 4% of total blocks found for 2013.
- Asic Miner – accounts for 4% of total blocks found for 2013. This

is a mining company where instead of mining yourself you buy shares of the company, and you make money through dividend earnings.

- Ozcoin – accounts for 4% of total blocks found for 2013. Features Double Geometric Payout with only 1% transaction fee.

For more mining pool listings and comparative studies, you may browse the web. If you want to know the most current developments in the Bitcoin economic landscape, you may also join online forums that discuss Bitcoins. CoinDesk usually has informative, relevant, unbiased articles. This will enable you to read even more of what everyone is talking about.

STAYING SAFE: AVOIDING SCAMS AND FRAUD

Bitcoin exists in the virtual world populated not only by caring and responsible 'netizens' who found a niche for themselves there, but also by tech savvy bigots out to disrupt the order and serenity of the flourishing virtual realm. They look for vulnerabilities to breach security protocols and deface websites. They steal your identities and use your credit card to make purchases for themselves, leaving your credit history in a shambles. They hack financial institutions and rob them of their money to enrich themselves. Worst, they do all these just to prove they are a breed apart from the rest of the internet citizenry, and that they are the lords and masters of the virtual realm.

It will be wishful thinking to expect that they will spare Bitcoin from their attacks. Fortunately, the Bitcoin system is so well designed that there never have been any major disruption which hindered its operation from the time the system was birthed in 2009. Of course, there are no perfect systems and hackers are always out there to prove this. Admittedly, there were security flaws and vulnerabilities in the Bitcoin system but they were always discovered early and corrected before hackers could exploit them.

As the largest distributed computing project on the internet, you would usually expect Bitcoin to have plenty of such weaknesses and be an easy target of hackers. Fortunately, Bitcoin's well-designed protocol and cryptography has made it almost impossible for hackers to shut down the system. It has, in fact, stood the test of time as is evident from its unblemished security track record.

Nevertheless, there is a continuous stream of reports citing massive losses of Bitcoins. In most instances, however, the losses are mainly due to the negligence of the users usually involving cases where the Bitcoin wallet files were lost, accidentally deleted, or hacked. Mounting reports of massive Bitcoin losses have also been noted, all of which have been attributed to hackers, scammers, and fraudsters.

Attacks on Bitcoin exchanges and other Bitcoin businesses have been on the rise lately - no thanks to the surging value of the crypto-currency in the market. Such incidents have become rampant, more frequent, and worrisome.

Bitcoin exchanges and other Bitcoin businesses have become fair game to hackers because they use third party Bitcoin software and other proprietary applications developed independently to promote Bitcoin trade with their services. And, like all other software, these proprietary client applications have inherent vulnerabilities that hackers love to discover and exploit.

If we are to gauge it from the increasing number of incident reports related to Bitcoin losses, it seems that the digital marauders are having a field day hacking Bitcoin wallets, dry feasting on the Bitcoin exchanges (which have become their favorite targets) and other Bitcoin businesses.

Like the hackers, the scammers and fraudsters are also having a field day capitalizing on the growing popularity of the crypto-currency by duping unsuspecting 'netizens' and robbing them of their hard-earned cash and Bitcoins. They establish fake Bitcoin exchanges or set up online businesses that accept Bitcoins for payments only to close shop promptly the minute someone starts questioning their legitimacy. They accept payments and/or deposits in Bitcoins and cash without delivering the promised goods or services.

Because of all these unfortunate incidents, a large cloud of doubt has fallen over Bitcoin as people have started developing negative notions about the Bitcoin ecosystem and on the integrity and safety of investing in it. The bottom line is none of these unfortunate incidents point to any vulnerability in the Bitcoin system itself. Its security protocols have remained intact and strong. And, notwithstanding the constant attacks from hackers, scammers, and fraudsters, the Bitcoin economy continues to flourish. The demand is rising and its rate doubling in value at an unbelievable pace.

As of current writing, a lot of investors want a slice of the Bitcoin pie, but they are being held back by such questions as - how can they stay safe in the face of the seemingly relentless hacking attacks? How can they protect themselves from being scammed and defrauded of their hard earned cash and Bitcoins?

There is only one answer to this – eternal vigilance. You need to actively participate in the various Bitcoin forums where you will get to know which company to deal and what Bitcoin services to use. It is in the forums where you will learn who not to deal with and which exchanges to avoid.

Here are some helpful tips on how you can stay safe and avoid being robbed or scammed:

- If you have a stash of Bitcoins in your possession, do not make the mistake of putting all of them in one place. Create at least two wallets (more if you have stashed quite a bit of fortune) – one wallet shall serve as your everyday wallet. This is what you will use for your day to day Bitcoin transactions which means it will be available most of the time. Make sure you keep the amount of Bitcoins in this wallet to a minimum. The other wallet(s) will serve as your vault or depository. This is where you will receive Bitcoin payments. You need to keep this wallet in a detachable drive like a USB stick and keep it somewhere safe. You should only access it or put it online only when it is necessary. Remember, hackers will only be able to hack wallets if they are stored in computers that are online. If the wallet is not accessible online, hackers won't be able to reach it and empty its contents. Don't worry because you can continue to add coins to it even if it is kept hidden somewhere safe, completely detached from your computer. All you need is to declare the network address of this wallet and people can send Bitcoins to it. In short, it will continue to accumulate Bitcoins even if it is kept out of reach of the prying eyes of scammers.
- Always back up your Bitcoin wallet files, and keep your backup files somewhere safe too. This way, you'd be able to recover the data if you accidentally erase your files or if your computer gets infected by a virus.
- Don't be tempted to use cloud services to store your Bitcoins. They are fair game and a favorite target of scammers nowadays.

Before dealing with an exchange or another Bitcoin business entity, you must do some due diligence work first. Get to know who the people are behind the company. Better still; get the physical address of the business if you can. Never deal with a company whose owners remain incognito. This way, you will have recourse if things turn sour.

BENEFITS AND DOWNFALLS OF BITCOIN

Everyone appears to have been bitten by the Bitcoin bug. The internet is buzzing with news and updates about it, and you'd be hard pressed to read an entire newspaper or financial magazine without stumbling on an article discussing its merits. More significant is the steady flow of precious capital from young entrepreneurs to fund Bitcoin start-ups.

Most notable among them is the $5 million investment made by Fred Wilson of Union Square Ventures to fund Coinbase, a startup that converts US dollars into Bitcoins and vice versa for a 1%transaction fee. (Union Square Ventures is a venture capital firm which invests on IT startups with high potentials for growth.)

Do you remember the Winklevoss twins of the Facebook fame (who claimed that Facebook was their original idea and not Zuckerberg's)? They too poured in $11 million hard currency to purchase Bitcoins, which left everybody's mouth gaping in amazement and wondering what is it they saw in Bitcoin that made them make such a determined move.

Here is what these young entrepreneurs saw – *the benefits that can be derived from the crypto-currency.*

- Untraceable transactions – Bitcoins can be sent peer to peer in total anonymity. Bitcoins are sent from one network address to another without anyone knowing whose addresses they are.
- Gives users full control – anyone can send or receive money anytime and anywhere in the world without limits and without the need of coursing it through a bank or any other financial

intermediary.

- The risk of inflation is low – Unlike most fiat currencies that can be printed at will and in volumes dictated by the issuing government, the quantity of Bitcoins that will be in circulation is fixed at no more and no less than 21,000,000, which means its purchasing power will be more stable.

- Very low or no transaction fees – Bitcoin transactions are processed with low or no transaction fees which makes it a superior choice because it will cost less to make payments compared to using credit cards, PayPal, or other online payment platforms.

- Secure payments, lower risk for merchants - With Bitcoins, merchants don't have to worry about fraudulent charge backs like they do with credit card or PayPal payments. Bitcoin transactions are also totally irreversible. Once payment is made, that's it.

- It requires no PCI compilation – as is required of merchants accepting credit card payments, so it also allows merchants to do business even in places where credit cards are not available. On top of that, it is tax free.

- Free from control or intervention by any central authority or government – With a cryptographically secure protocol, Bitcoin cannot be controlled or manipulated by anyone or any entity. It is also transparent with all the information about it embedded on the block chain. It is neutral allowing everyone to view, verify, and use it anytime in real time.

- Can be carried anywhere – You can bring along a million dollars worth of Bitcoins with you inconspicuously because they will easily fit onto a memory stick. This is something you can't do with hard cash or gold.

There are always two sides to a coin (pun slightly intended), which means if there are benefits, there must be some downfalls too. For Bitcoin, the downfalls are as follows:

- Limited Acceptance (at least currently) – The list of commercial establishments that directly accepts Bitcoin payments is still small although it is growing at a steady rate. The limited number of Bitcoin establishments dissuades many consumers from dipping into it, which can slow its growth.

- Untraceable – This is both a benefit and a disadvantage. People love it because they can send payments without it being traced back to them. This means, in the hands of shady individuals, it provides them the opportunity to purchase drugs or fund illicit trade without it being traced back to them.

- Highly Volatile – with a limited number of Bitcoins in circulation today faced by an increasing demand for it, the value of Bitcoins can fluctuate like crazy, fueled by even the smallest event or the weirdest market development.

Competing Crypto Currencies – Bitcoin may be the only virtual currency for now that has attained an acceptable level of success, but there is always a possibility that other crypto-currencies may pop out in the future and become more successful than Bitcoin.

CONCLUSION

I want to personally Thank You again for reading this book!

I sincerely hope the information contained will help you to understand the basics of the digital currency of the future: Bitcoins. In an ever-evolving global economy, it's easy to see the benefits of this crypto-currency, while also recognizing the possible pitfalls. The best idea is to keep yourself abreast of the information, and staying well-informed of the technology and logistics behind this game-changing digital currency of the future.

The next step is to put into practice the knowledge and employ the strategies we've discussed here to begin making Bitcoins work for you and your future!

Finally, if you enjoyed this book, please take the time to share your thoughts and post a positive review on Amazon. I would greatly appreciate your support!

Thank you and good luck!
Benjamin Tideas

(Additional Resources – Next Page)

ADDITIONAL RESOURCES

Please point your web browser to
www.plaid-enterprises.com/bitcoin
for more resources, my full bibliography and to grab your FREE book!

COPYRIGHT NOTICE